100 AMAZING FACTS ABOUT THE OLYMPIC GAMES

Summary

"Strength does not come from physical ability. It comes from an indomitable will."

— Mahatma Gandhi

Introduction

Dear reader, welcome to a fascinating journey through history, triumph, innovation and the indomitable spirit of humanity. You hold in your hands a book that tells 100 amazing facts about the Olympic and Paralympic Games, moments that defined and shaped what it means to be an athlete, and even more, a human being.

The stories you'll find in this book are stories of people who pushed the boundaries of what's possible, incredible records that were set and broken, and events that forever changed the face of the Olympic and Paralympic Games. From the first Olympic stadium to the first woman to carry the Olympic flag, from the athlete who ran with a prosthesis to the athlete who won without an opponent, every fact is a celebration of humanity in all its diversity and resilience.

As you go through this book, you'll discover stories of heroism, courage, determination, and pride, stories that transcend sport to touch on something much bigger. These stories are the essence of what it means to be an Olympian: to be a symbol of hope, progress and unity for the whole world.

So, dear reader, prepare to be inspired, moved and captivated. Get ready to discover a world of dreams come true, broken barriers, and moments that have made history. Take me on this journey through 100 incredible facts about the Olympic and Paralympic Games. You're ready? So, let's get to it.

Marc Dresgui

Fact 1 - The cradle of the Games: Ancient Olympia

You love the modern Olympic Games, don't you? But did you know they started a long, long time ago? Let's go back in time to 776 BC. in Greece, in a small town called Olympia.

At that time, the Greeks began to organize a sports competition in honor of Zeus, the king of the gods. These ancient Games, as they are called today, were not only a sporting event, they were also a great religious festival!

Sports back then were a little different. For example, there was a race called the stadion, which was a simple run of about 192 meters. It's a bit like our 200-meter runs today, but without the running shoes!

And the most incredible thing is that these Games lasted more than 1000 years! They finally ended in 393 AD. before being reinvented in 1896 in the form of the modern Olympic Games you know. What an incredible story, isn't it?

Fact 2 - Why Games every 4 years?

Have you ever thought about why the Olympic Games are held every four years? This tradition dates back to the very first Olympic Games of antiquity. It is inspired by what the ancient Greeks called an "Olympiad".

In ancient times, an Olympiad was a four-year period, used by the Greeks as a means of counting time. They named these periods after the winners of the stadion races at the Olympic Games.

The Games themselves were held in the first year of each Olympiad, meaning that the Games were held every four years. The ancient Greeks attached such importance to these Games that they used them to measure time!

When the modern Olympic Games were created in 1896, the organizers decided to keep this ancient tradition. So that's why you have to wait four years between each Olympic Games. Now you understand why this wait always seems so long!

Fact 3 - Olympic Games to honor Zeus

Have you ever heard of Zeus, the king of the gods in Greek mythology? It was to him that the first Olympic Games were dedicated! Rather surprising, isn't it? But let me tell you why.

Zeus, with his powerful lightning and throne on Mount Olympus, was the most important of the Greek gods. To honor him, the Greeks organized a great sports festival in Olympia, where there was a huge temple dedicated to Zeus.

But it wasn't just races and struggles. The Olympic Games were also a time of prayer and sacrifice for Zeus. Animals were sacrificed and large banquets were held in his honour.

So when you look at the Olympics today, don't forget that they started as a big party to honor Zeus. No wonder the performances are sometimes worthy of the gods, are they?

Fact 4 - The marathon: a heroic tribute

You've probably heard of the marathon, this incredibly long race of 42.195 kilometers! But do you know why it exists? It is actually a tribute to an ancient Greek hero. Sit back, the story is thrilling.

Long ago, in 490 BC, Greece was at war with Persia. According to legend, a Greek messenger called Phidippides ran from the city of Marathon to Athens to announce a great Greek victory over the Persians.

Phidippides would have covered this distance without stopping, and after delivering his message of victory, he would have died of exhaustion. A real feat, isn't it? But beware, even if this story is famous, some think it is more legend than reality.

When the modern Olympic Games were established in 1896, the marathon race was added in memory of the heroic feat of Phidippides. So every time you see a marathon, you witness a tribute to this ancient Greek hero!

Fact 5 - When the Olympic Games made their comeback

Just imagine: centuries have passed since the end of the ancient Olympic Games in 393 AD. Do you think all hope was lost for the Games? Well, no! Let me tell you how they made their comeback.

We owe this return to a French man named Pierre de Coubertin. In the 19th century, he dreamed of bringing back the Games to promote physical education and unity among nations. What a great idea, isn't it?

So he worked hard to convince the world of his vision. And finally, in 1896, the first modern Olympic Games were held in Athens, Greece, with 14 nations and 241 athletes. Not as many as today, but it was a fantastic start!

So the next time you watch the Olympics, think of Pierre de Coubertin. Without him, we might not have these incredible Games to meet every four years. Isn't that surprising?

Fact 6 - The Fastest Man: Usain Bolt

Have you ever dreamed of being the fastest in the world? One man has made this dream come true: Usain Bolt. He ran so fast that he was nicknamed "the Lightning". Ready to discover its incredible story?

Usain Bolt was born in Jamaica and started racing at an early age. His talent was so great that, at the age of 15, he won a gold medal at the World Junior Championships. Already impressive, isn't it?

But it was at the 2008 Olympic Games in Beijing that Bolt really caused a sensation. He broke the 100-meter world record with a mind-boggling time of 9.69 seconds. Then, at the 2012 Olympic Games in London, he improved this record even further, with a time of 9.63 seconds!

So every time you run, think about Usain Bolt. Maybe one day you too can break an Olympic record! What a race to history, isn't it?

Fact 7 - Michael Phelps: The King of Pools

Do you like swimming? Well, there's one man who's proven he's really the king of pools: Michael Phelps. His story is simply astonishing. Are you ready to dive into his universe?

Michael Phelps was born in the United States and started swimming as a little boy. His talent was so great that he participated in his first Olympic Games at only 15 years old, in 2000. That's already remarkable, isn't it?

But it was during the 2008 Olympic Games in Beijing that Phelps became a true legend. He won 8 gold medals, a record for a single Olympic Games! In total, he won 23 Olympic gold medals, a record that still stands.

So the next time you find yourself in a pool, think about Michael Phelps. With hard work and determination, who knows? Maybe you, too, could become an Olympic legend one day. Unbelievable, isn't it?

Fact 8 - Nadia Comăneci: gymnastic perfection

Just imagine: getting the perfect score of 10.00 in gymnastics at the Olympic Games. Sounds impossible? One athlete has achieved this feat: Nadia Comăneci. Ready to be amazed by his story?

Nadia Comăneci was born in Romania and started gymnastics at the age of 6. Her talent was so evident that only eight years later she was competing in her first Olympic Games. Impressive, isn't it?

But it was during the 1976 Olympic Games in Montreal that Nadia achieved the unthinkable. She achieved the first perfect score of 10.00 in the history of the Olympic Games in gymnastics, and this at only 14 years old!

Whenever you watch gymnastics, think of Nadia Comăneci. His performance showed the world that perfection is possible. She is a true inspiration for all gymnasts, and proof that the impossible can become possible. Isn't that wonderful?

Fact 9 - Usain Bolt breaks the 100m world record

Remember Usain Bolt, the fastest man in the world we talked about earlier. Do you want to know more about the day he broke the 100-meter world record? So, hang on, it's going to go very fast!

It was during the 2008 Olympic Games in Beijing. Bolt was already known as an incredible sprinter, but that day he would become a legend. He was ready to run the 100 metres, the fastest race of the Games. Exciting, isn't it?

At the gunshot, Bolt rushed with impressive speed. He covered the distance in an incredible time of 9.69 seconds, breaking the previous world record. Unbelievable, isn't it?

Now, every time you see a 100-meter run, think of Usain Bolt. He showed the world how fast a human can be. A real flash, isn't it?

Fact 10 - Bob Beamon's phenomenal leap

Have you ever dreamed of flying? A man named Bob Beamon turned that dream into reality, at least for a few seconds during the 1968 Olympics. Are you ready to jump into his incredible story?

Bob Beamon, an American athlete, competed in the long jump event in Mexico City. He was already a formidable jumper, but that day he was going to make a leap literally out of the ordinary. That's pretty exciting, isn't it?

In turn, Bob picked up his momentum, ran and jumped. But instead of an ordinary jump, it made such a huge leap that the judges had to measure the distance using a tape measure because their electronic instrument could not reach that distance. Bob jumped 8.90 meters, a record that stood for 23 years!

So next time you jump, think about Bob Beamon. He showed the world how far a human can jump. Unbelievable, isn't it?

Fact 11 - The Golden History of the Olympic Rings

Have you ever seen the five colorful Olympic rings? They are emblematic symbols of the Olympic Games. Do you want to discover their fascinating history? So, follow me on this colorful journey!

These five rings were created by Pierre de Coubertin, the founder of the modern Olympic Games. Each ring represents a continent: America, Europe, Africa, Asia and Oceania. That's pretty cool, isn't it?

They are intertwined to symbolize unity and friendship among all the nations of the world. The colors of the rings - blue, yellow, black, green and red - with the white background, include all the colors that appear on all national flags. Fascinating, isn't it?

So whenever you see these rings, remember their meaning. They represent the unity, friendship and competitive spirit of the Olympic Games. A beautiful symbol for an incredible event, isn't it?

Fact 12 - The fantastic journey of the Olympic flame

Have you ever heard of the Olympic flame? It is an important tradition that symbolizes the spirit of the Olympic Games. Ready to follow his fascinating journey? So, let's ignite the flame of knowledge!

The Olympic flame is lit in Olympia, Greece, from a parabolic mirror that uses the sun. It is then transported to the host country of the Games by a series of torchbearers. Can you imagine the trip?

But that's not all! It must remain lit throughout its journey to the Opening Ceremony of the Games. There, it is used to light a large cauldron that burns for the duration of the Games. What a strong symbol, isn't it?

The next time you see the Olympic flame, think about its incredible journey. It symbolizes the spirit of the Olympic Games: unity, peace and human effort. What a beautiful tradition, don't you think?

Fact 13 - Opening Ceremonies

Do you like big shows? Then you'd love the opening ceremonies of the Olympic Games. Ready to dive into this world of dazzling colors and performance? So, let's put on a show!

Each opening ceremony is a showcase of the host country. There are dances, songs, and sometimes even incredible demonstrations of technology! It is a way for the host country to show the world its culture and talents. Fascinating, isn't it?

And that's not all. There is also the parade of athletes from all participating countries, the Olympic oath and of course, the lighting of the Olympic cauldron with the flame that traveled from Greece. What an exciting time!

Next time you watch an opening ceremony, imagine all the work and preparation behind this incredible show. This is the beginning of an event full of emotions, challenges and triumphs. This is the beginning of the Olympic Games. Impressive, right?

Fact 14 - The secrets of Olympic medals

Have you ever dreamed of winning an Olympic medal? These precious awards are the ultimate symbol of sporting excellence. Ready to discover their secrets? So, let's go!

Each host country of the Games is responsible for creating the medals. Usually made of gold, silver and bronze, they are all specially designed to represent the culture and history of the host country. That's pretty cool, isn't it?

But do you know the secret of gold medals? Well, they are not entirely golden! Since 1912, gold medals have been mainly silver, covered with a thin layer of gold. Surprising, isn't it?

So the next time you see an athlete receive an Olympic medal, remember all the fascinating details behind those shiny records. They are much more than rewards, they are the symbol of dedication, talent and Olympic spirit. Unbelievable, right?

Fact 15 - The Olympic pigeon that thwarted the plans

Have you ever heard of the pigeon that disrupted the Olympic Games? No? Get ready to discover an unusual story that will surprise you!

It was in 1900, in Paris. For the first time, live pigeon shooting was introduced as an Olympic sport. The athletes had to slaughter as many pigeons as possible. A bit weird, isn't it?

But the most amazing thing is that a particularly reckless pigeon managed to escape the shooters and fly into the air, causing panic among the spectators! What chaos it must have been!

This anecdote highlights how the Olympic Games have evolved over time. Today, respect for animals is a core value of the Olympic Movement and no animals are injured in competitions. And luckily, isn't it? So, next time you watch the Olympics, think of that brave pigeon that managed to thwart the plans of this strange competition!

Fact 16 - Underwater Games: diving at 60 m

Are you ready to dive into an incredible story about the Olympic Games? So, hang on to your snorkel, because we will descend 60 meters below the surface of the water!

At the Olympic Games in Paris in 1900, a very special diving event took place. It wasn't about speed, it was about depth. Divers had to go as deep as possible. Intriguing, isn't it?

The man who won this competition was Charles Devendeville. He managed to dive to an incredible depth of 60 meters! Can you imagine what that looks like? It's like stacking 12 buses on top of each other!

Unfortunately, this event was not selected for the following Games. But the next time you jump into a pool, imagine diving as deep as Charles Devendeville. Impressive, right?

Fact 17 - The world record for throwing a laptop

Javelin throw, discus throw, hammer throw... But have you ever heard of the mobile phone launch? It is a competition that really exists, even if it has never been an Olympic event!

The idea is simple: participants should throw a mobile phone as far as possible. It's not a joke, it's a serious sport in some countries. Unbelievable, right?

The world record holder is a Finn named Tom Philipp Reinhardt. In 2014, he managed to launch a phone at an impressive distance of 136.75 meters! It's almost as long as a football field!

Even though mobile phone throwing is not an Olympic event, it is a great example of how people like to push their limits and invent new competitions. So the next time you're upset about your phone, don't throw it away. You could become a world champion!

Fact 18 - The amazing story of the Paralympic Games

Did you know that the Olympic Games are not the only ones to celebrate sportsmanship? Indeed, there are also the Paralympic Games, which are just as exciting and inspiring!

The Paralympic Games were born after the Second World War to help injured veterans reintegrate into society through sport. The man who came up with this brilliant idea was Ludwig Guttmann. He was convinced that sport could help rebuild lives.

The first of these Games was held in 1948, with 16 paraplegic veterans competing in archery. Over the years, the Paralympic Games have grown and now welcome athletes from around the world, competing in a wide variety of sports.

Thus, the Paralympic Games show the world that no matter what obstacles you face, with courage and determination, you can always aim for gold. Isn't that an incredibly inspiring lesson?

Fact 19 - Skiing on one leg: a Paralympic feat

Have you ever been skiing? If so, you know how difficult it is to keep balance, even with two legs. Now imagine skiing with only one leg. Unbelievable, right?

In the Paralympic Games, there is a category called standing alpine skiing, where athletes with various motor disabilities demonstrate incredible control and balance to hit the slopes at full speed.

One particularly impressive athlete is the Swiss Michael Brügger. Despite losing his right leg in a motorcycle accident, he won several gold medals at the Paralympic Games, hurtling down the slopes with only one leg and unfailing determination.

These Paralympic athletes are proving that with courage, determination and a lot of training, you can achieve things that many would consider impossible. So, next time you think of a challenge as impossible, remember skiing on one leg!

Fact 20 - Armless archers aim for gold

Do you remember the last superhero movie you saw where the archer shoots arrows with incredible accuracy? Now imagine if this archer didn't have an arm. Unthinkable? Not at all!

At the Paralympic Games, armless archers mastered the art of archery with their feet. They lie on their backs, hold the bow with their feet, and use their mouths to pull the rope. Yes, it's as impressive as it sounds.

One of these archers is Matt Stutzman from the United States, nicknamed the Archer without arms. Born without arms, he holds the world record for the longest accurate target in archery, at an incredible distance of more than 300 meters!

These athletes show us that no matter the obstacles, you can always go for gold. It's a reminder that nothing is really impossible if you put your mind to work and work hard.

Fact 21 - The courage of the first Olympic woman

Do you know the story of the first woman to participate in the Olympic Games? Her name was Hélène de Pourtalès and she was as brave as a lioness.

Born in 1868, Hélène de Pourtalès was part of the Swiss sailing team at the 1900 Paris Olympic Games. At that time, women were generally not allowed to participate in the Games, but Helen did not let that stop her.

The sailing team she sailed on won the gold medal, making Hélène the first woman not only to compete in the Olympic Games, but also to win a medal! Think about this the next time you feel like something is impossible.

Hélène de Pourtalès broke the barriers for all the female athletes who followed. Thanks to her courage and determination, girls around the world know that they too can be Olympic champions.

Fact 22 - The Women's Era: The 2012 Olympic Games

Do you remember the 2012 Olympic Games in London? It was at these Games that history was rewritten by female athletes.

For the first time in the history of the Olympic Games, each participating country sent at least one woman to the competition. This meant that there were women from all corners of the world, representing their countries with pride and strength.

It was also the first time that all sports had women's events. Traditionally male sports, such as boxing, have opened their doors to women, showing that girls can be as strong and competitive as boys.

In summary, the 2012 Olympic Games were a great victory for gender equality in sport. So, to all the girls reading this, remember: you can be whatever you want, and no one can tell you otherwise!

Fact 23 - The veil in the ring: Sarah Attar's story

Can you imagine running a marathon with a veil? That's exactly what Sarah Attar did in 2012. This Saudi-American athlete made history at the London Olympics.

Sarah was one of the first two women to represent Saudi Arabia at the Olympic Games. Despite London's warm climate and veil, Sarah ran the entire marathon. A real feat!

She may not have won the race, but she gained something far more important: the respect and admiration of the whole world. By defying climate and stereotypes, Sarah has proven that sport is for everyone, regardless of gender or dress.

Her story is an inspiration to all the girls and women of the world. Like Sarah, never forget that you are capable of achieving great things, despite the obstacles that stand in your way.

Fact 24 - Discover Curling: The Sport of Broom on Ice

Curling, a broom sport on ice? Yes, you heard right. This winter Olympic discipline is often nicknamed "ice chess".

Invented in Scotland in the sixteenth century, curling is played on an ice rink. Teams throw granite stones at a target, while scanning the ice to control the stone's trajectory. This is where brooms come into play!

The brooms are not there to clean the ice, but to warm it slightly. This creates a thin layer of water that allows the stone to slide more easily. It's quite an art!

So the next time you watch the Winter Olympics, think about those curling athletes. Not only do they have to have incredible strength to throw stones, but also great accuracy to sweep ice properly. A real challenge!

Fact 25 - BMX Olympic stunts

Have you ever seen cyclists fly? With BMX, it's possible! These athletes perform breathtaking aerial stunts, and it's all part of the Olympic Games.

Born in the 70s in California, BMX was influenced by motocross. Young cyclists began to imitate the jumps and stunts of their motorized idols on specially designed bikes, and BMX was born.

BMX made its debut at the Olympic Games in 2008 in Beijing, and quickly won over the public with its fast races and daring stunts. Each race features eight riders who compete on a course strewn with obstacles, jumps and sharp turns.

Next time you watch the Olympics, keep an eye out for BMX events. You will be impressed by the speed, agility and courage of these athletes. It's cycling, but not like you've ever seen it!

Fact 26 - Modern pentathlon

Can you imagine running, swimming, shooting, fencing and riding horses, all in one competition? This is exactly what modern pentathlon athletes do at the Olympic Games!

The modern pentathlon was created by Pierre de Coubertin, the founder of the modern Olympic Games. He wanted a sport that "tests a man as a whole", mixing physical endurance and technical mastery. Modern pentathlon made its debut at the Games in 1912.

Each athlete competes in five disciplines: fencing, swimming, horseback riding, pistol shooting and running. These are varied disciplines that test different aspects of the athlete's skill and endurance. It is a real challenge to excel in all these areas.

Next time you watch the Olympics, check out the modern pentathlon. You will be impressed by the variety of skills and endurance required to participate in this unique event.

Fact 27 - From pyramids to rings

Have you ever wondered where the next Olympic Games will take place? Prepare to be surprised: Egypt, the land of pharaohs and pyramids, is the next guest!

For the first time in history, the Middle East will host the Olympic Games. Egypt, a country known for its ancient history and iconic archaeological sites, will be the focus of global attention.

Cairo, the Egyptian capital, is already preparing its infrastructure to welcome athletes and spectators from around the world. Imagine watching competitions with the pyramids of Giza in the background. It is a show that promises to be unforgettable.

The organisation of these Olympic Games marks an important milestone for Egypt and for the Middle East. It is an opportunity for these regions to show their culture, hospitality and passion for sport. See you at the Olympic Games in Cairo!

Fact 28 - Beijing 2008: A giant bird's nest for the Games

Have you ever seen a bird's nest? How about a giant bird's nest that can accommodate 91,000 people? The Beijing 2008 Olympic Games brought the majestic "Bird's Nest" to the world.

The "Bird's Nest", officially called the Beijing National Stadium, was the architectural star of the Games. Designed by Swiss architects Herzog & de Meuron, its unique design resembles a woven bird's nest, hence its nickname.

Not only did the stadium host the opening and closing ceremonies of the Games, but it was also the scene of many sporting achievements. It was there that Usain Bolt set his world record in the 100 meters.

Today, the "Bird's Nest" remains an icon of Beijing, attracting tourists from all over the world. It continues to host sporting events and concerts, keeping alive the atmosphere of the Olympic Games. A real proof that the Olympic spirit lives on long after the end of the Games.

Fact 29 - Tokyo 2020: The Games of the Digital Age

Have you ever imagined an Olympic Games in the digital age? This is what Tokyo 2020 presented to the world. With a global pandemic underway, these Games have innovated in technology and participation.

The organizing committee used artificial intelligence to translate in real time into more than 11 languages. Virtual reality allowed spectators around the world to experience the Games as if they were there. The robots, on the other hand, helped in various tasks, ranging from cleaning to assisting spectators.

Athletes have also benefited from digital innovation. Performance monitoring devices were used to improve their training. In addition, for the first time, eSports were showcased, revolutionizing the traditional notion of Olympic sport.

Tokyo 2020 has shown that the future of the Olympic Games could be digital. It ushered in a new era of participation and innovation, proving once again that the Olympic Games are much more than just a sporting competition.

Fact 30 - The Olympic Values

Do you know the core values of the Olympic Games? There are three of them: union, excellence and respect. Each plays an essential role in the philosophy of this international competition.

Unity is the ability to bring together athletes and nations from around the world every four years, creating a sense of belonging and solidarity. The Olympic Games symbolize global harmony, promoting intercultural dialogue and mutual understanding.

Excellence does not only mean winning medals, but also surpassing oneself. It is the aspiration to give the best of oneself, on and off the field. Athletes aim not only for victory, but also for personal development, balance between body, mind and soul.

Finally, respect encompasses fair play, integrity and friendship. Respecting the rules, the opponents, the judges, and oneself is a fundamental aspect of the Games. This value educates athletes to be better athletes, but also better citizens.

These values embody the spirit of the Olympic Games, which goes beyond mere sporting competition.

Fact 31 - The Olympic Truce

Did you know that the origin of the Olympic Games is linked to a period of sacred peace in antiquity? This is the Olympic Truce, a fascinating concept that persists to this day, despite modern times.

In ancient Greece, for the duration of the Games, all wars were suspended. Greek states laid down their weapons to allow athletes and spectators to travel and participate safely in the Games. It was a time of unity, respect and celebration of culture and sport.

Over the centuries, this tradition has been somewhat lost, but in 1992, the International Olympic Committee revived the idea of the Olympic Truce. Today, the aim is to promote peace and global understanding through sport, for the duration of the Olympic Games and beyond.

While it is difficult to silence all hostilities around the world, the Olympic Truce remains a powerful symbol of what the Games represent: a time when humanity can come together in peace to celebrate sporting excellence.

Fact 32 - Sport and peace: the Olympic spirit

Do you know the deep philosophy behind the Olympic Games? Beyond competition and records, the Olympic spirit conveys fundamental values that include peace and harmony among peoples.

The central idea is simple: sport has the power to transcend cultural, political and social differences. The Olympic Games are a global event where athletes, regardless of their origin, share the same stadium, the same Olympic Village, in a spirit of equality and mutual respect.

Baron Pierre de Coubertin, the founder of the modern Olympic Games, saw sport as a powerful tool for promoting peace and international understanding. For him, the main thing was not to win, but to participate.

The Olympic spirit is the deep belief that, despite our differences, we can come together, compete in a spirit of fair play and celebrate humanity as a whole. It is a lesson in unity and peace that the world desperately needs to remember.

Fact 33 - The athlete who ran for his life

Have you ever come across the story of Guor Marial? An athlete who not only ran for a medal, but for his life. Born in the midst of South Sudan's civil war, Marial lived a life of challenges and tragedies from an early age.

Forced to work in a labor camp at the age of eight, Marial managed to escape. His escape was a literal race for survival, which turned into a passion for running. Without adequate equipment or training, Marial persisted, running barefoot over rough terrain.

In 2012, Marial won the right to participate in the London Olympic Games. With no nation to support him – South Sudan did not yet have an Olympic committee – he raced as an independent athlete under the Olympic flag.

Marial's story is more than a sports story. It is a reminder of the strength of the human spirit, the power of sport as an escape and the beauty of a race fought not for glory, but for freedom.

Fact 34 - The glasses that won gold

Have you ever heard of Dick Fosbury? Not only did he revolutionize the high jump with his "Fosbury Flop", but he was also the first to wear glasses while jumping. Yes, you read that right, glasses!

In 1968, during the Olympic Games in Mexico City, Fosbury astonished the world with his unprecedented technique. Instead of jumping belly down as was the norm, he jumped with his back to the bar. And he did this while wearing glasses. It was unusual, but effective.

His feat not only won gold, but also allowed athletes requiring glasses to gain confidence. Fosbury has proven that glasses are not an obstacle, but can be an asset. And that's not all: his jumping technique has since been adopted by jumpers around the world.

Fosbury's eyewear is not just a fashion accessory or necessity, it is an integral part of his legacy. Through them, he paved the way for many athletes to no longer feel limited by their sight.

Fact 35 - The swimmer without a country

Can you imagine swimming for your life and then swimming for a medal at the Olympic Games? Yusra Mardini did it. This Syrian swimmer has become a symbol of hope and determination for thousands of refugees around the world.

Born in Damascus, Yusra had to flee war-torn Syria in 2015. During its perilous crossing of the Aegean Sea, the boat's engine failed. Without hesitation, she and her sister jumped into the water and pushed the boat, saving the lives of 18 people.

Arriving in Germany, Yusra continued to train despite the difficulties. Her talent and perseverance earned her a spot on the Refugee Olympic Team in 2016. In Rio, she swam not for one country, but for all the refugees in the world.

Yusra Mardini's story is more than a sports story. It is a testimony of courage, hope and the strength of the human spirit. It is proof that even in the most difficult situations, humans can achieve extraordinary things.

Fact 36 - Records broken by mother athletes

Being a mother is an achievement in itself, but imagines becoming a mother while breaking world records. Incredible women have proven that motherhood and elite sport are not incompatible.

Take Kim Clijsters as an example. After giving birth to her daughter in 2008, she made a sensational return to the tennis courts and won the US Open in 2009 and 2010. She is the only mother to have won a Grand Slam since 1980.

Then there's Jessica Ennis-Hill, the British heptathlete. After giving birth to her son in 2014, she won gold at the World Championships in Athletics the following year. A feat rarely accomplished by athletes after motherhood.

And let's not forget Serena Williams, who, after the birth of her daughter in 2017, continued to dominate the tennis world. These women are inspiring examples that prove that motherhood can be a source of strength, not an end to a sporting career.

Fact 37 - The oldest gold medalist in history

Age is often considered a determining factor in high-performance sports. Yet some athletes prove otherwise. One of them, a real phenomenon, is Oscar Swahn, the oldest gold medalist in history.

Swahn was a Swedish shooter who made his Olympic debut at the age of 60, at the 1908 Olympic Games in London. He won the gold medal in two events, becoming the oldest gold medalist in history at the time.

However, this was only the beginning of his impressive Olympic career. Swahn competed in two more Olympic Games, in 1912 and 1920. At the age of 72, at the 1920 Games, he won a silver medal, becoming the oldest Olympic medalist of all time.

Oscar Swahn's story reminds us that sport is not just about youth and physical vigor. It's also about determination, discipline and passion. At any age, Olympic gold is within reach of those who dream big.

Fact 38 - The youngest Olympian

At the opposite end of the age spectrum of Olympic athletes, you will find the surprising case of Dimitrios Loundras, the youngest Olympic athlete in history. Born in 1885 in Athens, he marked the annals of sport by his precocity and talent.

Loundras was only 10 years and 218 days old when he competed in the 1896 Olympic Games in Athens. He was a member of the Greek parallel gymnastics team that won the bronze medal. Yes, you read that right, he was only 10 years old!

His outstanding performance at such a young age is a record that remains intact to this day. No other athlete so young has ever competed in an Olympic Games since.

The story of Dimitrios Loundras is proof that age is just a number when it comes to achieving excellence. Young and old, Olympic athletes continue to amaze us with their determination, talent and passion for sport.

Fact 39 - The marathon runner who ran the wrong way

Imagine yourself at the start line of the marathon of the 1908 Olympic Games in London. At the signal, you launch with determination. However, one of the competitors, Dorando Pietri, became famous for a completely different reason than victory.

Pietri, an Italian athlete, found himself in the lead as he approached the finish, but exhausted, disoriented, he took the wrong path in the finish stadium. It collapsed several times, and despite the help of officials to get up, it arrived the wrong way.

Despite his chaotic arrival, Pietri crossed the finish line first, but was disqualified for receiving help. The victory was awarded to American marathon runner Johnny Hayes.

His courageous, if misguided, journey has gone down in Olympic history, a reminder that determination and effort can sometimes count as much as leadership. Dorando Pietri is the symbol of the athlete who, even in confusion and exhaustion, never gives up.

Fact 40 - The diver who fell 10 stories

Do you know the story of Alain Bernard, the miraculous diver? In 1983, this Frenchman survived a fall of 33.5 meters, the equivalent of ten floors, during a high-flying diving competition.

Alain had misjudged his jump and landed on his stomach, which, at such a height, is comparable to hitting concrete. An icy silence had fallen on the audience at the sight of this terrifying fall.

Incredibly, despite the violence of the impact, Alain survived. He was quickly rescued and taken to hospital, suffering multiple fractures, including several ribs and his sternum, but his prognosis was not life-threatening.

This impressive fall did not prevent Alain Bernard from returning to high-flying diving. It's a powerful reminder of athletes' resilience, and that even after the most terrifying falls, it's still possible to get up and jump again.

Fact 41 - When fencing became a dance

Have you ever noticed the grace of fencers in full competition? It is fascinating to know that fencing, once a means of defense, has evolved into a delicate and strategic dance.

Fencing began as a military combat technique in the Middle Ages. But over time, deadly duels were replaced by sports competitions, and fencing began to feel more like a dance than a fight.

This is due to the importance of accuracy, timing and coordination in modern fencing. Each movement must be perfectly executed, just like in a dance. The fencer must be in constant balance, ready to attack or parry at any time.

So the next time you're watching a fencing match, take a moment to admire the intricate choreography going on. Fencing is not just a sport, it is a dance, a real symphony of blades.

Fact 42 - The gymnast who flew... without arms

Do you know Jennifer Bricker? This incredibly talented American gymnast managed to reach the top, and this, without the use of her arms. Yes, you read that right.

Jennifer was born with a rare condition called upper limb agenesis, which means she was born without arms. However, that never stopped her from pursuing her dreams. On the contrary, she used this as motivation to prove that nothing is impossible.

Using her feet and body in innovative ways, Jennifer was able to master the complex movements of gymnastics, including somersaults and rotations. His performances have become a source of inspiration for people around the world.

His motto, "Everything is possible", is a testament to his courage and determination. Jennifer Bricker is living proof that even the greatest obstacles can be overcome with will and courage.

Fact 43 - Around the World in 80 Games

When it comes to the Olympic Games, Paris is undoubtedly a city that quickly emerges in the mind. Do you know why? Not only has it hosted the Games twice, but in 2024 it will host them a third time, marking an important milestone in Olympic history.

The very first event, in 1900, was integrated into the Universal Exhibition. It was marked by several firsts, including the introduction of women into the Games. Unfortunately, these games were somewhat chaotic, with competitions spread over more than 5 months.

In 1924, the Games made a triumphant return to Paris. This time they were much better organized and became a model for future Olympic events. The Opening Ceremony, as we know it today, began with these Games.

And now, with the 2024 Games in sight, Paris is once again preparing to welcome the world. This time, the city promises an unforgettable Olympic experience, aligning the events with the iconic monuments of the French capital.

Fact 44 - When the Games came home

Did you know that London has hosted the Olympic Games three times? But it is undoubtedly the 2012 Games that remain etched in the collective memory. In fact, London was the first city to host the Games for the third time, after 1908 and 1948.

In 2012, the Olympic Stadium, located in the Queen Elizabeth Olympic Park, became the beating heart of the city. With a capacity of 80,000 people, it was the scene of exceptional performances and unforgettable emotions.

Among the highlights, we remember the grandiose opening ceremony orchestrated by director Danny Boyle. A vibrant blend of British history and culture, it captivated the world and set the tone for a spectacular Games.

Finally, the outstanding performance of the British team, which finished third in the medal standings, made the London 2012 Games an unforgettable event for the nation. These Games truly marked a triumphant return home.

Fact 45 - Rio's incredible transformation for the Games

Have you heard about the dramatic transformation Rio de Janeiro underwent for the 2016 Olympic Games? As the first city in South America to host this major event, the stakes were high and the expectations from around the world immense.

In the race to host the Games, Rio has drawn up an ambitious plan to modernize its city. The construction of the Barra Olympic Park was one of the most impressive projects, transforming a suburban district into a true sports metropolis with state-of-the-art facilities.

The transformation didn't stop there. The city's transport network has undergone a major modernization with the extension of the metro and the creation of a new express bus system. Rio's efforts have improved access and mobility for its residents and thousands of visitors.

The impact of the Games is not only measured in terms of infrastructure, but also in terms of legacy. The legacy of the Rio Games can be seen in the hope and pride they inspired in Brazilians, marking a new milestone in the history of this vibrant tropical city.

Fact 46 - The Woman Who Challenged Hitler at the Games

Do you know the story of the athlete who challenged Hitler at the Berlin Olympics in 1936? Let me tell you Helene Mayer's inspiring story.

Born in Germany, Mayer was a talented fencer. Despite her Jewish roots, she was selected to represent Nazi Germany, a political choice calculated by Hitler's regime to hide its anti-Semitism from the world.

During these Games, Mayer won silver for the German team. However, her most memorable moment came when she bravely raised her hand in an Olympic salute, not a Nazi salute as Hitler would have wished. This gesture was interpreted as a silent challenge to the Nazi regime.

Helene Mayer remains a symbol of resistance and courage. Despite the pressures and injustices of the time, she was able to preserve her integrity and demonstrate to the world the importance of equality and humanity in sport, a lesson that still resonates today.

Fact 47 - The city that has hosted the Games twice

Do you know the only city that has had the honour of hosting the modern Olympic Games twice? This is London, the vibrant capital of the United Kingdom.

The first time was in 1908. The Games were originally scheduled to take place in Rome, but an eruption of Mount Vesuvius forced them to be moved. London rose to the challenge and staged the Games in just 10 months, setting new standards for the event, including the official marathon distance at 26.2 miles.

More than a century later, in 2012, London became the first city to host the Olympic Games for the second time. With the Queen Elizabeth Olympic Park at the heart of the Games, London has delivered spectacular events and left a lasting legacy for the city.

Whether by chance or choice, London has twice demonstrated its ability to welcome the world, celebrating the Olympic spirit of competition, excellence and unity in diversity.

Fact 48 - The story of the Refugee Olympic Team

Maybe you're not aware of the existence of the refugee Olympic team. Yes, you heard right. Since the 2016 Olympic Games in Rio de Janeiro, this exceptional team has competed under the Olympic flag.

Initially composed of 10 athletes from different countries and practicing different sports, it has allowed people displaced by war and persecution to compete on the world stage. Their participation highlighted the challenges faced by refugees around the world.

At the Tokyo 2020 Games, the team nearly tripled to 29 athletes. All have stories of displacement, resilience and determination that put a human face on the global refugee crisis.

The Refugee Olympic Team embodies the spirit of Olympism, demonstrating that sport has the power to bring hope and change, even in the most difficult circumstances. Their courage and perseverance are an inspiration to all.

Fact 49 - When football became Olympic

Did you know that football wasn't always an Olympic sport? In reality, football made its official entry into the Olympic Games in 1900 in Paris, but without a formal tournament structure.

At first, the sport was not as universally recognized as it is now. In these first Games, only three teams - Great Britain, France and Belgium - participated. Great Britain won the first-ever Olympic football match.

It was not until 1908 that football became a structured competition at the Olympic Games, with a knockout tournament system. It was again the British who won the gold medal that year, asserting their dominance over the sport.

Today, Olympic football is a major event, with 16 men's and 12 women's teams from around the world competing for gold. The sport has come a long way since its humble Olympic beginnings, but its essence remains the same: the love of the game.

Fact 50 - The History of Pole Vaulting

Do you know the origin of the pole vault? Dating back to ancient times, this sport was used by Greek soldiers to jump over natural obstacles. It was at the 1896 Olympic Games that it was introduced as an official discipline.

At first, pole vaulting was not as you know it today. The jumps were performed with solid wooden poles, making the sport more dangerous and unpredictable. It wasn't until 1957 that pole vaulting experienced a revolution, with the introduction of fiberglass poles.

The adoption of this material has radically changed the sport. Athletes were able to reach previously unimaginable heights, thanks to the flexibility and resilience of fiberglass. The current record is 6.18 meters, held by Armand Duplantis since 2020.

From now on, pole vaulting is one of the most spectacular and anticipated disciplines of the Olympic Games. It perfectly illustrates the constant evolution of sport, where innovation and human ambition are constantly pushing the limits.

Fact 51 - The gymnast who made the spinning top

There are stories that compel admiration, and this gymnast's is one of them. Elena Mukhina, an exceptional Soviet gymnast, had a remarkable talent for rotations. His specialty? The tricks in the air, which she performed with disconcerting ease.

Elena Mukhina had developed such a mastery of rotation that she literally seemed to fly. She innovated with a particularly complex and risky figure, the "Salto Thomas". However, the execution of this figure ultimately had disastrous consequences. In the run-up to the 1980 Olympic Games in Moscow, she was seriously injured during training, leaving her paralyzed.

Despite her tragic accident, Elena Mukhina remained a prominent figure in gymnastics. His determination and bravery in the face of adversity inspired many athletes. It is a symbol of the total dedication that high-performance sport requires, but also of the risks it can entail.

Elena Mukhina's story is a poignant reminder of the need to balance ambition and security in sport. She remains in our memories as the gymnast who could not stop turning, and who paid a high price for her passion.

Fact 52 - The man who swam faster than a shark

Imagine yourself for a moment at the start line of a swim race. Your opponent is none other than one of the fastest predators in the oceans: the shark. This is the challenge that Michael Phelps, the most successful swimmer in the history of the Olympic Games, took on in 2017.

As part of a special episode of "Shark Week" on the Discovery Channel, Phelps competed against a great white shark over a distance of 100 meters. He wasn't literally swimming next to the shark, of course. The two performances were recorded separately and then superimposed using augmented reality technology.

Even though Phelps, aided by a special suit and monofin, swam at an impressive speed, the white shark eventually got ahead of him. The shark finished the race in 36.1 seconds, while Phelps posted a time of 38.1 seconds.

Despite his defeat, Phelps showed the world how exceptional human capabilities can be. Swimming almost as fast as a shark is a feat that only an athlete of his calibre could achieve. And even if you don't swim faster than a shark, remember that every small victory counts in the pursuit of your own goals.

Fact 53 - The Amazing History of the Winter Games

To know the history of the Olympic Games is also to explore the history of the Winter Games. Did you know that winter sports were originally included in the Summer Games? Yes, you read that right. It was at the 1908 Games in London that figure skating made its first appearance.

The idea of separating the Summer Games from the Winter Games originated in 1921, when the International Ice Hockey Federation proposed including hockey and speed skating in the Games. The decision was made, and it was in 1924, in Chamonix in France, that the first Winter Games were born, bringing together 258 athletes from 16 different nations.

Since then, these Games have been held every four years, like their summer counterparts, but delayed by two years. They have grown rapidly and have become the go-to global winter sports event, with a variety of disciplines, ranging from alpine skiing to bobsleigh.

So the next time you watch the Winter Games, you'll know a little bit more about their origin. And who knows? Perhaps you will be inspired to try your luck in one of these exciting winter disciplines.

Fact 54 - The Man Who Won Gold on One Leg

Do you know that physical limits can be transcended by will and passion? The story of this Olympic athlete proves it. His name: Oliver Halassy, a Hungarian swimmer who won not one, but three gold medals, all on one leg.

Halassy was born in 1909 in Hungary. At the age of 10, he lost his left leg in a streetcar accident. But that didn't stop him from pursuing his passion for swimming. Using only the strength of his right leg and arms, he developed a powerful and effective swimming technique.

He participated in three Olympiads (1928, 1932, 1936), winning three gold medals and one silver in water polo. Yes, you read that right, water polo, a sport that requires excellent mobility and great strength in the legs.

Oliver Halassy's story is a lesson in resilience and courage. Despite his disability, he not only competed but dominated an Olympic discipline, proving that limits are often those you set for yourself.

Fact 55 - The weightlifter who lifted an elephant

Have you ever heard of Louis Cyr, the man recognized as the strongest in the world at his time? Born in Quebec in 1863, Cyr was not only a renowned weightlifter, but also a true legend for his extraordinary prowess, including "lifting" an elephant.

At an exhibition in Boston in 1895, Cyr managed to support the weight of a four-ton elephant on his back during a public performance. This fact, while unbelievable, nevertheless requires clarification. In reality, Cyr placed himself under a platform on which the elephant was mounted, and resisted the enormous mass of the animal.

This feat is one of Cyr's many accomplishments that have astonished the world. He set several incredible strength records, such as lifting 500 pounds (227 kg) with one hand and a 433-pound (196 kg) barrel with his fingers.

The story of Louis Cyr is an example of extreme physical strength and human endurance. He proved that training and determination can enable an individual to reach heights of almost inconceivable feats.

Fact 56 - The craziest relay race of all time

Can you imagine an Olympic event so chaotic that almost all teams are disqualified? This is exactly what happened during the 4x100-meter relay race at the 2008 Summer Olympics in Beijing.

During this memorable race, three of the eight teams were disqualified for dropping the stick or passing out of the transmission zone. The British team dropped the stick, the Americans went out of the zone, as did the teams of Nigeria and Brazil.

In the face of this chaos, the Jamaican team, led by Usain Bolt, flew over the race to win gold with a new world record. The Japanese team won silver and Canada was awarded the bronze medal after all these disqualifications.

This race has been remembered as one of the craziest in the history of athletics. It proves that even at this level of competition, the unpredictability of sport can still prevail, offering spectacle and unexpected surprises.

Fact 57 - When the Games went green

Do you know the story behind the first "green" Olympic Games in history? It was in 2012, in London, that the Olympic Committee decided to focus on sustainability and ecology.

The main site, the Olympic Park, was a dilapidated former industrial area in London's East End. The organizers transformed this site into a beautiful green space, using recycled materials to build the stadiums and creating new habitats for local wildlife.

The London 2012 Olympic Games were also marked by sustainable transport initiatives. Dedicated bus and bicycle lanes were created, and spectators were encouraged to get to the sites using public transport or walking.

These games have left a lasting legacy, transforming a neglected part of London into a vibrant and sustainable space. It also set a new standard for future Olympic Games, highlighting the importance of integrating sustainability into the planning and implementation of events of this magnitude.

Fact 58 - Roller skiing: an Olympic discipline?

You like skiing, but you don't have snow? No problem! Roller skiing, also known as roller skis, could be the solution. It is very similar to cross-country skiing, except that it is practiced on asphalt instead of snow. And you know what? It has even been considered as an Olympic discipline.

The roller ski first appeared in the 1930s in Europe. Since then, it has become a popular way for cross-country skiers to train during the summer months. Roller skis are very similar to cross-country skis, but instead of sliding on snow, they ride on small wheels.

In the 2000s, it was proposed to include roller skiing in the Summer Olympics. However, despite the support of some athletes and organizations, it has not yet been officially accepted as an Olympic discipline.

So even if you can't compete for a gold medal in roller skiing yet, it's still a great way to enjoy the outdoors and keep fit year-round. Who knows? Maybe you'll see roller skiing at the Olympics in the near future.

Fact 59 - Athletes who became movie stars

Some Olympic athletes have a second life after their sports career. And for some, it's in the Hollywood spotlight. Do you wonder who are these athletes who have gone from the track to the canvas? Let me enlighten you.

Johnny Weissmuller is probably the most famous of all. An Olympic swimming champion, he won five gold medals at the Olympic Games in the 1920s. After retiring from sport, he found new success playing the character of Tarzan in a series of films in Hollywood.

Bruce Jenner, now known as Caitlyn Jenner, is another Olympic athlete turned movie star. A gold medallist in the decathlon at the 1976 Olympics, Jenner became a television personality and starred in several films and television series.

Esther Williams, a competitive swimmer who never competed in the Olympics because of World War II, went on to star in a series of Hollywood blockbusters, showcasing her swimming skills. So even if you're an Olympic champion, don't limit your dreams to the track or the pool. Hollywood might call you one day.

Fact 60 - The history of Olympic mascots

Olympic mascots have become a tradition since the Grenoble Games in 1968. But do you know how they were born and what their role is? It's a story as colorful as the mascots themselves.

The very first Olympic mascot was Schuss, a small character on skis for the Winter Olympics in Grenoble. But it was Waldi, the dachshund of the Munich Games in 1972, who was the first official mascot of the Summer Olympics. Since then, each host city has created its own mascot, often related to the local culture.

Mascots play a crucial role in promoting the Games. They create an emotional connection with the public, especially children, and are a way to share the spirit of the Games. Mascots are present on merchandise, promotional posters and are often used in opening and closing ceremonies.

From Cobi, the cubist dog of Barcelona in 1992, to Miraitowa and Someity, the futuristic characters of Tokyo 2020, Olympic mascots have brought joy and entertainment to the Games, while symbolizing the Olympic spirit. They are an integral part of the legacy of the Games.

Fact 61 - The strangest shoes

When you think of sports equipment, you probably imagine outfits designed for comfort and performance. But did you know that some Olympic shoes have defied these expectations, becoming as iconic as the athletes who wore them?

The first pair you need to know is that of Abebe Bikila. At the 1960 Rome Olympics, the Ethiopian marathon runner ran barefoot to win gold simply because his new shoes hurt. Four years later, he won gold again, but this time with shoes!

At the 1972 Games in Munich, American Frank Shorter ran the marathon in a pair of neon yellow shoes, the only one of its kind at the time. These shoes not only attracted attention, but they also helped Shorter win gold.

Finally, at the 2008 Games in Beijing, American swimmer Michael Phelps wore shoes designed especially for him by Speedo. They were intended to improve blood circulation after races. These examples show that in the Olympic arena, even shoes can make history.

Fact 62 - The heaviest gold medal in history

Have you ever imagined the weight of an Olympic gold medal around your neck? Did you know that not all gold medals carry the same weight? You may be surprised to learn that the heaviest gold medal in Olympic history was awarded at the Vancouver 2010 Games.

These medals, designed by Canadian artist Corrine Hunt, weighed an average of 500 to 576 grams, depending on the discipline. Each medal was unique and contained designs inspired by British Columbia First Nations culture.

In comparison, the standard gold medal for the Summer Olympics weighs about 396 grams, while the Winter Games usually weighs between 470 and 576 grams. The Vancouver medals were therefore exceptionally heavy.

So the next time you see an athlete receive a gold medal at the Olympic Games, think about the extra physical effort they had to put in to carry that extra weight around their neck. It is indeed an additional symbol of their strength and determination.

Fact 63 - Games that never took place

Do you know the Olympic Games that never happened? These are the 1916, 1940 and 1944 editions. Indeed, these Games were cancelled because of the two world wars that ravaged the world during these periods.

The 1916 Games were supposed to be held in Berlin, but World War I decided otherwise. As for those of 1940, they were planned in Tokyo, then moved to Helsinki, before finally being canceled because of the Second World War.

The same fate befell the 1944 Games, which were to be held in London. Despite efforts to maintain the event, the ongoing war made the task impossible.

This is how these three editions of the Olympic Games went down in history as "The Games That Never Happened". Further proof of the profound impact of global conflicts on all aspects of life, including sport.

Fact 64 - The Incredible Jamaican Bobsleigh Team

Do you know the history of the Jamaica bobsleigh team? A tropical country that has decided to compete in a winter sport is unusual to say the least, isn't it?

In 1988, this Jamaican team, made up of athletes from the sprint, caused a sensation by qualifying for the Olympic Winter Games in Calgary, Canada. The initiative came from two Americans who saw potential in the speed of Jamaican sprinters.

Despite initial mockery and makeshift equipment, the team showed unwavering determination. Their participation in the Games was marked by a spectacular accident, but they earned the respect and admiration of the world for their courage and perseverance.

In this way, Jamaica's bobsleigh team was able to highlight a fundamental aspect of the Olympic spirit: it is not so much the result that counts, but the courage to participate, to dare and to push the limits of what is possible. A real message of hope, isn't it?

Fact 65 – The basketball team that scored 100 points

Can you imagine a basketball team scoring 100 points in a single game? This is exactly what happened on March 2, 1962 at an NBA game in the United States.

The feat was accomplished by Wilt Chamberlain, then a player of the Philadelphia Warriors, in a game against the New York Knicks. Chamberlain scored a staggering 100 points, setting a record that remains unmatched to this day in the NBA.

But what's even more impressive is that Chamberlain accomplished this feat without the help of the three-point line, which wasn't introduced until 1979. He scored 36 baskets on 63 shot attempts and converted 28 of his 32 free throws.

The story of this achievement illustrates the essence of sport: pushing the boundaries of what is possible. She continues to inspire generations of athletes to excel, dream big and aim high. Maybe you, too, are ready to score your own "100 points" in life?

Fact 66 - The tennis player who played for 11 hours

Can you imagine playing a tennis match for 11 hours? Not one player, but two men, John Isner and Nicolas Mahut, achieved this stunning feat at Wimbledon in 2010.

The match, which took place over three days, went down in history as the longest tennis match ever played, with a total duration of 11 hours and 5 minutes. The last set alone lasted 8 hours and 11 minutes, a record in itself.

In the end, it was the American John Isner who ended up winning the match with a mind-blowing last set of 70 to 68. The exhaustion was such that a ten-minute break was necessary after the match to allow the players to recover.

The tenacity, endurance and pure competitive spirit demonstrated by these two athletes that day marked the history of the sport. Their feat is a reminder that limits are made to be pushed back, even if it takes 11 hours.

Fact 67 - The boxer who won with one hand

Have you ever heard of Paul Pender? This American boxer became a sensational phenomenon when he won a fight in 1961, despite a broken hand.

In the sixth round, Pender fractured his right hand. Many would have given up at this point, but not Pender. He continued to fight with one hand, showing incredible determination.

Using mainly his left hand for his attacks, Pender defied all expectations and managed to hold on for the next nine rounds. His impeccable defensive technique and ability to counter his opponent's attacks allowed him to win.

This impressive feat remains a source of inspiration for boxers around the world. Pender showed that with determination and courage, you can overcome even the toughest challenges in the ring.

Fact 68 - One stadium per 100,000 people

Have you ever imagined what a stadium with a capacity of 100,000 people could look like? The Azteca Stadium in Mexico City is this mythical place. Its construction for the 1970 FIFA World Cup was an architectural feat.

Designed by architect Pedro Ramírez Vázquez, this colossal stadium was built in 1966. It can accommodate more than 100,000 spectators, making it one of the largest stadiums in the world. Its name refers to the ancient Aztec civilization of Mexico.

The Azteca Stadium is one of the few stadiums in the world to have hosted two FIFA World Cup finals. The first in 1970, where Brazil triumphed over Italy, and the second in 1986, where Argentina beat West Germany.

This iconic structure remains a source of national pride for Mexico. More than just a gathering place for football fans, Azteca Stadium is a symbol of the country's dedication and passion for the sport.

Fact 69 - The highest Olympic stadium in the world

Have you ever heard of the world's tallest Olympic Stadium? Located in La Paz, Bolivia, the Hernando Siles Stadium sits at an impressive altitude of 3637 meters above sea level.

Inaugurated in 1931 and able to accommodate more than 41,000 spectators, this stadium has witnessed many sporting achievements, but also difficulties inherent in its location. The altitude is so high that athletes often have difficulty breathing, which can affect their performance.

It is also a double-edged sword for Bolivia's local football team. While Bolivian players are used to extreme conditions, their opponents are often weakened by lack of oxygen, giving the home team a considerable advantage.

The Hernando Siles Stadium is a perfect example of how geography can influence sport. Despite the challenges he presents, he remains an icon in the world of sport and a symbol of pride for the Bolivian people.

Fact 70 - The birth of the Youth Games

Have you ever heard of the Youth Olympic Games? Created in 2010, these games aim to inspire athletes aged 14 to 18 and compete at a high level of skill.

The idea of this competition germinated in the mind of Jacques Rogge, then President of the International Olympic Committee (IOC). Its aim is to promote sport and the Olympic spirit among young people, while offering them a unique multicultural experience.

The first Youth Games were held in Singapore in 2010. They are hugely successful, with 3,600 athletes from 204 countries participating. The Games include summer and winter events, similar to the traditional Olympic Games.

Since then, the Youth Olympic Games have become an important springboard for young sporting talent. They represent the future of the Olympic Games, fostering education, respect and friendship through sport.

Fact 71 - The first Winter Games: Chamonix 1924

Have you ever thought about the origin of the Olympic Winter Games? In fact, they were born in 1924 in Chamonix, France. Known at the time as the "International Winter Sports Week", they did not gain recognition as the Winter Olympic Games until 1926.

This first edition brings together 258 athletes, including 11 women, representing 16 different nations. The program has 16 events: from figure skating to cross-country skiing to bobsleigh. Surprisingly, ice hockey, although already popular, made its debut at the Olympic Games at this edition.

Scandinavian athletes dominated these first Winter Games. For example, Thorleif Haug of Norway won three gold medals in cross-country skiing. However, the local heroes, the French bobsleigh team, won gold, triggering a real party in the host city.

Today, these first Winter Games are considered the beginning of an important sporting tradition, celebrating the spirit of competition and camaraderie in snowy landscapes around the world.

Fact 72 - When the rain stopped beach volleyball

You probably have the image of beach volleyball as a sport played under a radiant sun, on a beach with warm sand. However, during the 2012 Olympic Games in London, rain disrupted this idyllic vision.

On July 29, the second day of the beach volleyball events, a sudden downpour hit the Horse Guards Parade, the historic site turned beach volleyball stadium. Umbrellas open in the stands, players fight against the elements as much as against their opponents.

The organizers plan to interrupt the matches, but eventually, the competition continues. The players, gliding and skidding in the wet sand, offer a unique and memorable show. The downpour turns the competition into an epic battle against the elements.

This day remains etched in Olympic history as a moment of challenge and resilience. Despite the deluge, beach volleyball continued, demonstrating that even the British weather cannot stop the Olympic spirit.

Fact 73 - The most played water polo match in history

You know water polo as an intense sport, but do you remember the most hotly contested match of all time? It was at the 1956 Olympic Games in Melbourne, a match that became famous as "Blood in the Water".

The political tension between Hungary and the Soviet Union, in the midst of the Suez crisis, found itself in the pool. This semi-final match was more than just a game, it represented a battlefield on which these two nations expressed their tensions.

The battle was fierce. The shots were as intense out of the water as they were inside. When Hungarian player Ervin Zador emerged from the pool, his face bloodied after a violent blow, the match was stopped. Hungary led 4-0, and were declared the winner.

This match has gone down in history as one of the fiercest ever played. More than just a game, it showed how political tensions can manifest themselves even in the heart of the Olympic Games.

Fact 74 - The heaviest judoka of all time

When you think of judo, you probably imagine slender athletes, but do you know the heaviest judoka of all time? His name is Ricardo Blas Jr., also known as "Little Mountain" from Guam.

Born in 1986, Ricardo Blas Jr weighed 218kg at the London 2012 Olympic Games, breaking the previous record of 200kg held by Swedish wrestler Anders Ahlgren in 1912. Despite his weight, Blas Jr showed impressive agility and speed on the tatami.

Blas Jr didn't win a medal in London, but he showed that judo, like many other sports, is not about size or weight, but about skill, technique and determination. He has remained an iconic figure in the sport of his home country, Guam.

So next time you think about the perfect fitness for a sport, remember Ricardo Blas Jr., the heaviest judoka of all time, who has defied stereotypes and inspired many athletes around the world.

Fact 75 - When archery became an Olympic sport

Archery is one of humanity's oldest skills, but did you know it took a while for it to become an Olympic discipline? It was in Paris, in 1900, that archery first appeared at the Olympic Games.

Despite its integration, archery was not an instant success. Indeed, due to a lack of uniform international standards, the discipline was removed from the Olympic programme after the 1920 Games. It was not until 1972, in Munich, that it regained its place.

Archer Neroli Fairhall of New Zealand made history in 1984 by becoming the first paraplegic athlete to compete at the Olympic Games against able-bodied athletes. Archery has always been an inclusive sport, open to all, regardless of physical ability.

So the next time you watch an archery competition at the Olympic Games, remember how far the sport has come to earn its place. Each arrow thrown is a reminder of the constant evolution of Olympism.

Fact 76 - The longest race of all time

Do you know the Self-Transcendence 3100 Mile Race ultra-marathon? It is the longest certified race in the world, and it takes place every summer in New York. Runners have 52 days to cover 3100 miles, or about 4989 kilometers.

This incredible race was created in 1997 by Indian philosopher Sri Chinmoy to challenge the limits of human endurance. He believed that surpassing oneself in physical effort allowed a better understanding of oneself.

The event takes place on a 0.5488-mile (883-meter) urban course in Queens. Riders must complete this circuit more than 5649 times to complete the race. They typically run 18 hours a day, eating and drinking while running.

In 2019, Finland's Ashprihanal Aalto set the race record in 40 days, 9 hours, 6 minutes and 21 seconds. As you put on your sneakers for your daily jog, think of those incredible athletes who run the equivalent of a marathon and a half every day for almost two months!

Fact 77 - The largest collection of Olympic medals

Do you know Michael Phelps? He is the most decorated athlete in the history of the Olympic Games, with an impressive total of 28 medals. His collection includes 23 gold, three silver and two bronze medals.

Phelps began his Olympic career at the Sydney Games in 2000, aged just 15. Despite his young age, he finished 5th in the 200m butterfly final, becoming the youngest male swimmer to represent the United States at the Olympic Games since 1932.

He won his first gold medal in 2004 in Athens, breaking the world record in the 400m individual medley. Thereafter, Phelps went on to dominate the Games, setting numerous world and Olympic records.

So next time you're at the pool, think about Phelps and his incredible determination. Maybe you won't reach his level, but who knows how far you can go if you set goals and work hard to achieve them?

Fact 78 - The athlete who ran with a prosthesis

Do you know Oscar Pistorius? This South African athlete became an emblematic figure of the London 2012 Olympic Games. He was the first amputee athlete to run at the Olympic Games, using specially designed carbon fiber prostheses, called "racing blades".

Born without fibula, Pistorius had both legs amputated below the knee when he was only eleven months old. He grew up playing many sports before devoting himself to athletics. In 2004, he won a gold medal at the Athens Paralympics in the 200m, setting a new world record.

In 2008, after a long legal battle, he won the right to compete alongside able-bodied athletes at the Olympic Games. Four years later, at the London Games, he reached the semi-finals of the 400m, marking a historic milestone for athletes with disabilities.

Thus, the story of Pistorius is a powerful lesson about overcoming obstacles. It reminds us that determination and courage can lead to unprecedented achievements.

Fact 79 - The first woman to carry the Olympic flag

Have you ever heard of Norma Enriqueta Basilio from Sotelo? This Mexican athlete made history at the Olympic Games in Mexico City in 1968. She became the first woman in the world to light the Olympic cauldron at the Opening Ceremony.

Enriqueta, a talented sprinter, was chosen for the role because of her athleticism and representation as a Mexican. His ascent of the 90 steps leading to the cauldron, carrying the Olympic flame, became an iconic moment of the 1968 Games.

Her gesture symbolized gender equality and paved the way for the growing participation of women in the Olympic Games. At the time, there were only 781 female athletes among the 5,530 participants in the Mexico City Games.

Enriqueta's act changed that. Her bold and historic gesture ushered in a new era for women in sport, proving that they have their place on the Olympic stage.

Fact 80 - The first women's Olympic competition

Have you ever heard of Hélène de Pourtalès? She made history at the 1900 Summer Olympics in Paris, becoming the first woman to compete in an Olympic event. You may be wondering what sport she played? The veil!

In 1900, sailing was introduced as an Olympic sport and Hélène, a member of the Swiss team, participated in the sailing event in the 1-2 ton class. Her team sailed on the yacht "Lérina" and won the gold medal, making her not only the first woman to participate, but also the first female Olympic gold medalist.

This first female participation was a turning point for the Olympic Games, even if women were still largely under-represented. It was not until 1928 that women were allowed to compete in athletics events.

Hélène de Pourtalès made history and paved the way for millions of women in sport. Her achievement helped demonstrate that women could compete at a high level in the world of sport.

Fact 81 - The athlete who refused his medal

Do you know that not everyone dreams of winning an Olympic medal? At the 1972 Munich Games, Swedish fencer Hans-Gunnar Liljenvall deliberately denied his bronze medal. What for? The reason is rather unusual.

Liljenvall, a member of Sweden's modern pentathlon team, had tested positive for alcohol during a doping control. Indeed, before the shooting competition, he had drunk two beers to calm his nerves. It was the first time alcohol tests had been conducted at the Olympics and Liljenvall's blood alcohol level exceeded the legal limit.

Because of this, the Swedish team was disqualified from the shooting event and lost points, which dropped the team to fourth place overall. However, after an appeal, they were reinstated and won bronze. Liljenvall, however, refused to accept the medal in protest.

The Liljenvall incident remains etched in history as a lesson in sporting integrity and underlines the importance of fair play in the Olympic Games.

Fact 82 - The Day Gymnastics Changed Forever

Are you a gym fan? Then you will probably remember July 18, 1976, the day when gymnastics changed forever thanks to a 14-year-old Romanian gymnast, Nadia Comaneci.

Comaneci became famous at the Montreal Olympics in 1976, where she achieved something incredible. In the middle of the competition, on the uneven bars, she performed such a perfect routine that the judges awarded her the first score of 10 in Olympic history.

The scoreboard was not even prepared for this, and displayed "1.00" instead of "10.00", as it was assumed that such a rating was impossible to achieve. But Comaneci proved the opposite and revolutionized the sport.

Nadia Comaneci scored a total of seven perfect marks during these Olympic Games, an achievement unmatched to date. She showed the world that perfection is attainable and forever changed the way gymnasts are judged.

Fact 83 - The team that won without playing

It may sound unbelievable, but there was a team that won an Olympic medal without even playing a single game. This happened during the 1904 Olympic Games in St. Louis, USA, and the team in question was the cricket team.

In 1904, only two teams were registered for the cricket tournament: the United States and Canada. However, Canada withdrew from competition just before the start of the games. Rather than cancel the event, organizers decided to declare the U.S. the winner by default.

Thus, without having played a single match, the United States cricket team ended up with a gold medal around its neck. Curiously, this would be the last time cricket would be included in the Olympic program.

This little-known fact remains a singular example in the history of the Olympic Games. This is an illustration of the flexibility required to organize an event of this magnitude, where surprises are always possible.

Fact 84 - The track speed record

You've probably heard about the incredible performances of track racers, but did you know who holds the track speed record? This is Jamaican sprinter Usain Bolt, a name that has become synonymous with lightning speed.

On August 16, 2009, at the World Championships in Athletics in Berlin, Bolt set a world record in the 100 metres in 9.58 seconds. This performance is equivalent to an incredible speed of 37.58 km/h. He remains to this day the fastest man on the track.

This phenomenal record is no coincidence. Bolt has always been known for his speed. Even growing up in Jamaica, he was already excelling in speed racing. His preparation, dedication and technique eventually brought him to this all-time record.

This performance remains one of the most memorable in the history of the sport. Bolt not only pushed human boundaries, but also demonstrated how preparation, determination and talent can lead to exceptional results.

Fact 85 - The tallest basketball player in history

Do you know the greatest basketball player of all time? This is Suleiman Ali Nashnush, who played for the Libyan national team in 1962. If you think today's professional basketball players are great, wait until you read how huge Nashnush was!

He measured a staggering 2.45 meters, which distinguishes him as the tallest basketball player in the history of the sport. Its size was the result of surgery to treat a disease of the pituitary gland.

This giant was not only a basketball player, but was also known for his role in the film "Fellini Satyricon", a 1969 Italian drama. His one-of-a-kind stature has made him famous far beyond the boundaries of basketball.

However, despite his extraordinary size, Nashnush did not have a long career in basketball. He nevertheless went down in history as the greatest player in the history of the sport. Proof that basketball, like many other sports, is full of surprises!

Fact 86 - Fastest Gold Medal

Do you know who won the fastest gold medal in the history of the Olympic Games? This distinction goes to American athlete Jim Hines, who achieved this feat at the Mexico City Games in 1968.

Hines ran the 100 metres in 9.95 seconds, becoming the first man to break the 10-second barrier in that event at an Olympic Games. He beat all his competitors with such speed that his feat was considered a pivotal moment in the history of athletics.

Beyond his outstanding performance, what makes Hines' record even more impressive is that it was set at a time when athletics tracks weren't as fast as they are today. In addition, today's shoes and equipment are significantly superior to those of Hines' time.

The fastest gold medal was therefore won in conditions that, compared to those of our time, were much less favourable. A great example of how sportsmanship can transcend human limitations!

Fact 87 - The Day Hockey Became Olympic

Remember the day ice hockey became Olympic? It was at the 1924 Winter Games in Chamonix that ice hockey made its first official appearance on the Olympic Winter Games programme.

Ice hockey's debut at the Olympic Winter Games was marked by Canadian dominance. The Canadians won the gold medal by defeating the United States 6-1 in the final. The Canadians, with their fast and technical game, laid the foundation for the sport internationally.

But ice hockey's entry into the Olympic fold was not without difficulty. Organizers faced considerable logistical challenges in preparing for the rink, which raised questions about the sport's viability for the Winter Olympics.

However, despite these initial difficulties, ice hockey survived and thrived. Since that first edition in Chamonix, sport has become one of the most popular and watched events of the Winter Games. It's a great story of perseverance and love of sport, isn't it?

Fact 88 - The first African team to win gold

Do you know the epic story of the first African team to win gold at the Olympic Games? It's a story that goes back to the Tokyo Olympics in 1964. It was Ghana's men's football team that made history.

The Ghanaian team, nicknamed the "Black Stars", showed unwavering determination throughout the tournament. Guided by their iconic captain, Aggrey Fynn, they defeated many favourites teams, proving that African football can compete with the best nations in the world.

The final against Czechoslovakia was an unforgettable match. Leading 1-0 in the first half, Ghana came back to score thanks to a goal from Fynn, before winning the match 3-2 after extra time. The victory was hailed as a big step forward for African football.

This Olympic gold medal marked the emergence of African football on the world stage. Since then, Africa has produced some of the most talented teams and players in the world, confirming the feat of the first African team to win gold.

Fact 89 - The day the Games became Paralympic

Have you ever heard of the fascinating story of the birth of the Paralympic Games? It all started in 1948, with a sporting event organized for World War II veterans suffering from spinal cord injuries. It was not until later, in 1960, that these games officially became Paralympic.

The original idea came from Dr. Ludwig Guttmann, a German neurologist exiled in England during the war. Convinced of the benefits of sport for the rehabilitation of his patients, he organized the first "Stoke Mandeville Games" at the hospital where he worked.

But it was in Rome in 1960, in parallel with the Olympic Games, that these games took on an international scope, welcoming 400 athletes from 23 countries. They were first called the "Paralympic Games", echoing the Olympic Games.

Since then, the Paralympic Games have been held every four years, right after the Olympic Games. These competitions are a testament to the incredible strength and resilience of athletes, going beyond what is thought possible, and proving that sport is much more than just competition.

Fact 90 - The story of the first Paralympic mascot

You may know the mascots of the Olympic Games, but did you know that the Paralympic Games also have their own mascots? The very first Paralympic mascot was introduced at the Seoul Games in 1988, and it was named "Nooly".

Nooly was conceived as a stylized little girl, symbolizing the image of a promising future. The organizers wanted a mascot that not only represents the Paralympic spirit, but also embodies the culture and spirit of Korea.

Nooly was created to convey a message of equality and harmony. Its name, a contraction of the Korean words "nool" (meaning "joy") and "ly" (meaning "all together"), perfectly sums up the philosophy of these games: joy shared by all, despite differences.

Since Nooly, each Paralympic Games has had its own mascot, each symbolizing a message of hope and inspiration. These mascots play an important role in making the Games more engaging and accessible, while highlighting the extraordinary determination of Paralympic athletes.

Fact 91 - The longest ski jump in history

You may have seen some impressive ski jumps, but do you know the absolute record? On March 18, 2017, it was Stefan Kraft, an Austrian ski jumper, who made the longest jump in the history of this sport.

That day, during a competition in Vikersund, Norway, Kraft flew down the track, defying the laws of gravity. With incredible launch speed, it managed to land at the staggering distance of 253.5 meters, setting a new world record.

He challenged the limits of human endurance and flight mechanics, making ski jumping not only a sport, but also a demonstration of precision and daring. It was carried by an irreproachable technique, a perfect body alignment and an incredible speed.

This leap remains etched in the annals, a feat that continues to inspire and amaze. Every time you see a jumper start, remember Kraft and his incredible record. Who knows how far the next jumpers can go?

Fact 92 - The marathon runner who ran without shoes

Can we imagine running a marathon without shoes? This challenge seems inconceivable to most of us, but one athlete took it up. Abebe Bikila, an Ethiopian runner, accomplished this incredible feat at the 1960 Olympic Games.

In Rome, Bikila showed up at the start line of the marathon without shoes. His choice was not a whim. In reality, the new shoes he had been provided with were too uncomfortable. So he decided to run as he used to do in Ethiopia, that is, barefoot.

He ran the 42.195 kilometers of the Olympic course on the asphalt of the Eternal City, braving the pains and difficulties. And the result? Not only did he finish the race, but he also won it, setting a new Olympic record in 2 hours 15 minutes and 16.2 seconds.

This exceptional performance by Bikila, a true lesson in courage and determination, is etched in the history of sport. Whenever you think of limits, remember that some are made to be challenged.

Fact 93 - The history of the fastest rugby team

If you think rugby is a slow sport, this story might change your mind. Do you know the All Blacks, the New Zealand national rugby union team? Not only are they famous for their war dance, the Haka, but they also hold a remarkable record.

At the 2015 Rugby World Cup, the All Blacks faced France in the quarter-finals. From the kick-off, New Zealand deployed a fast, powerful and precise game. Their strategy? Use speed to destabilize the opposing defense.

Result? They scored a total of 9 tries during this match, establishing a final score of 62-13. But it's not the score that's most impressive, it's the speed at which they scored. The All Blacks scored their first try just 1 minute and 38 seconds into the game.

Thus, this team has proven that rugby is not only about brute force, but also about speed and agility. A great game lesson for all oval ball enthusiasts!

Fact 94 - The first woman to win five gold medals

You certainly know some big names in women's sport, but have you ever heard of Fanny Blankers-Koen? This Dutch athlete was the first woman to win five gold medals at the Olympic Games in a single edition!

Born in 1918, Fanny took up athletics at an early age. When she competed at the London Olympics in 1948, she was already an accomplished athlete. But no one expected what she would accomplish during these games.

Competing in four events – the 100 metres, 200 metres, 80 metres hurdles and 4x100 metres relay – Fanny dominated every race. Despite doubts about her age and the fact that she was already a mother of two, she proved to be a force to be reckoned with.

With her incredible performance, Fanny Blankers-Koen not only broke records, but also stereotypes about female athletes of the time. Her victory paved the way for generations of female athletes and changed the face of sport forever.

Fact 95 - The history of the first Olympic stadium

You have certainly admired the great modern Olympic stadiums, but do you realize that it all started with the Panathenaic Stadium in Athens? It was in this historic stadium that the first modern Olympic Games were held in 1896.

Originally built in 330 BC for the Panathenaic Games, this stadium was renovated in marble by architect Lycurgus in 144 BC. With a capacity of 50,000 spectators, it was and remains an architectural masterpiece.

For the first modern Olympic Games, the stadium was renovated and modernized, while retaining its original design. It was here that the 14 participating nations competed in a variety of sports, ranging from athletics and cycling to swimming and gymnastics.

The Panathenaic Stadium laid the foundation for all future Olympic stadiums. It remains a strong symbol of the Olympic spirit and the history of sport. It continues to host events, continuing the legacy of the Olympic movement.

Fact 96 - The first Arab woman to win a gold medal

Maybe you don't know her yet, but Hadiya Darwish made Olympic history. This incredible woman is the first Arab athlete to win a gold medal.

Hadiya, born in Morocco, won gold at the 1984 Olympic Games in Los Angeles, in the 400-meter hurdles. She defended the colours of her country with unparalleled determination, breaking down cultural and sporting barriers.

His victory was not only a personal achievement, it paved the way for Arab and Muslim athletes around the world. Darwish has become an inspiration to generations of athletes who have followed in his footsteps, breaking stereotypes and challenging prejudice.

Hadiya Darwish's gold medal did more than win a race, it changed the face of sport for Arab and Muslim women. She remains today an icon for all women who fight for their place in the world of sport.

Fact 97 - Gold medal won without opponent

Believe it or not, there is a case where an Olympic gold medal has been won without a single opponent showing up. The story takes place during the 1904 Olympic Games in St. Louis, and the athlete in question is George Eyser.

George Eyser was an outstanding German-American gymnast, known for winning six medals in a single day, despite a wooden leg. However, perhaps his most surprising achievement was winning gold in an event in which he was the only participant.

The event was the individual all-around on apparatus, a gymnastic discipline that combines several exercises. Eyser carried out his routines without an opponent to challenge him, measuring himself only against himself and the judges' expectations.

This singular victory is a reminder that, in the Olympic Games, every story is unique. Even if you may think it's less impressive to win without an opponent, remember that every athlete, like George Eyser, must first and foremost surpass himself.

Fact 98 - The athlete who won with a somersault

Dick Fosbury's name is etched in the annals of athletics, thanks to a revolutionary technique he invented and used to win gold at the 1968 Olympic Games in Mexico City. His victory is a perfect illustration of how a single individual can change the conventions of his sport.

Fosbury introduced a whole new approach to high jump, now known as the "Fosbury Flop". Instead of passing the belly bar first, as was the custom at the time, he took a bold approach of jumping back first, with a characteristic rotation resembling a somersault.

This unconventional leap was initially met with skepticism. But when Fosbury won Olympic gold by setting a new record, the perception changed dramatically. Soon, his innovative technique became the norm in the high jump.

So the next time you watch a high jump competition, remember that every jump is proof of Fosbury's bold innovation. He transformed his sport and proved that there are no limits to creativity in athletics.

Fact 99 - Dean Hall's denim swimsuit

Can you imagine swimming in jeans? That's what Dean Hall, an American long-distance swimmer, did. His challenge was not just to swim, but to break a world record by doing it in jeans. His feat not only changed the perception of clothing in the swimming world, but also inspired thousands.

Dean started swimming to fight his leukemia cancer. He decided to set himself a challenge and chose to swim in jeans to raise awareness for his cause. He trained intensively and eventually managed to achieve his goal of swimming 132 miles (212.43 kilometers) in the Willamette River in the United States.

During his feat, he not only achieved his distance goal, but also managed to break the world record for the longest distance ever swum in open water. He accomplished all this while wearing jeans, defying the usual expectations and standards of competitive swimming.

Dean's story shows that obstacles can be overcome, no matter what their nature. He remains an inspiration to all those facing challenges, in sport and beyond.

Fact 100 - The Day the Olympic Spirit Conquered the World

Have you heard of when the Olympic spirit really took off? It was during the opening ceremony of the Barcelona Olympics in 1992. This event not only marked the history of the Games, but also captured the hearts of the world.

Spanish Paralympic archer Antonio Rebollo lit up the night with his flaming arrow. Tasked with lighting the Olympic cauldron, he succeeded in his shot from 70 meters away, and the Olympic flame shone, symbolizing the spirit of perseverance, unity and peace. This gesture moved millions of people around the world.

This memorable moment was more than just a symbolic act. He proved that the Olympic Games are an event that unites the whole world, across borders, cultural differences and personal challenges. It was the perfect example of the Olympic spirit, which is what makes this event so special.

The Opening Ceremony of the Barcelona 1992 Games will go down in history as the day when the Olympic spirit truly conquered the world. An eternal reminder of what it really means to be an Olympian.

Conclusion

That's it, dear reader, you've just completed an incredible journey through 100 amazing facts about the Olympic and Paralympic Games. From the first woman to carry the Olympic flag to the athlete who turned down her medal, you've been able to discover stories of courage, perseverance and Olympic spirit that have defined these global competitions.

These stories are not only historical facts, they are witnesses to humanity's resilience, its ability to overcome obstacles, break down barriers and push the boundaries of what is possible. They are a celebration of the human spirit, a proof that when we come together for sport, we can achieve great things.

The Olympic and Paralympic Games remind us that no matter where we come from, gender or disability, we all have the ability to achieve great things.

As I conclude this book, I wish you, dear reader, to keep these stories in mind and draw inspiration from them. May they serve as a reminder that each of us has the potential to achieve great things, to defy the impossible, to make history. And who knows, maybe one day you'll be part of those stories. After all, the Olympic and Paralympic Games are much more than sporting competitions, they are a celebration of humanity in all its glory.

Marc Dresgui

Quiz

1) Which woman was the first to carry the Olympic flag at the Opening Ceremony?

a) Babe Didrikson Zaharias
b) Wilma Rudolph
c) Fanny Blankers-Koen
d) Norma Enriqueta Basilio Sotelo

2) Which country hosted the first women's Olympic competition in 1900?

a) France
b) Greece
c) United States
d) Germany

3) Which athlete refused his medal at the 1968 Olympic Games?

a) Tommie Smith
b) John Carlos
c) Peter Norman
d) Muhammad Ali

4) Who revolutionized gymnastics with its somersault?

a) Olga Korbut
b) Nadia Comăneci
c) Simone Biles

d) Larisa Latynina

5) Who is the athlete who set the track speed record at the Olympic Games?

a) Usain Bolt
b) Michael Johnson
c) Carl Lewis
d) Jesse Owens

6) Who is the greatest basketball player in the history of the Olympic Games?

a) Michael Jordan
b) Shaquille O'Neal
c) Yao Ming
d) Gheorghe Mureșan

7) Who is the first athlete to win five gold medals at the Olympic Games?

a) Jesse Owens
b) Paavo Nurmi
c) Emil Zatopek
d) Larisa Latynina

8) Where was the first Olympic stadium built for the modern Games?

a) Athens, Greece
b) Paris, France
c) London, England

d) Berlin, Germany

9) Who is the first Arab woman to win an Olympic gold medal?

a) Nawal El Moutawakel
b) Hassiba Boulmerka
c) Hoda El-Korashi
d) Sarah Attar

10) Which athlete has won a gold medal without an opponent at the Olympic Games?

a) Jesse Owens
b) Carl Lewis
c) Paavo Nurmi
d) Walkover in Cricket, 1900

11) Who is the marathon runner who ran and won without shoes?

a) Kipchoge Keino
b) Abebe Bikila
c) Eliud Kipchoge
d) Wilson Kipsang

12) Which rugby team holds the record for the fastest win?

a) New Zealand
b) South Africa
c) Australia

d) France

13) Who is the swimmer who broke the world record while wearing jeans?

a) Michael Phelps
b) Mark Spitz
c) Ian Thorpe
d) Fred Bousquet

14) What was the day the Olympic Games conquered the world?

a) Opening of the Athens Games in 1896
b) Opening of the Berlin Games in 1936
c) Opening of the Los Angeles Games in 1984
d) Opening of the London 2012 Games

15) Who is the first African team to win a gold medal at the Olympic Games?

a) Kenya
b) Ethiopia
c) South Africa
d) Nigeria national football team, 1996

16) Who is the first Paralympic mascot?

a) Paraly
b) Ato
c) Lyo
d) Schneemann

17) What is the record for the longest ski jump in history?

a) 230m
b) 243m
c) 251.5m
d) 263m

18) When did ice hockey become an Olympic discipline?

a) 1908
b) 1920
c) 1932
d) 1948

19) When were the Paralympic Games officially recognized?

a) 1960
b) 1972
c) 1984
d) 1992

20) Which team has won a competition without even playing?

a) United States national basketball team, 1960
b) Uruguay national football team, 1924
c) Great Britain Cricket Team, 1900
d) Canada Ice Hockey Team, 1924

Answers

1) Which woman was the first to carry the Olympic flag at the Opening Ceremony?

Correct answer: d)Norma Enriqueta Basilio Sotelo

2) Which country hosted the first women's Olympic competition in 1900?

Correct answer: (a)France

3) Which athlete refused his medal at the 1968 Olympic Games?

Correct answer: b)John Carlos

4) Who revolutionized gymnastics with its somersault?

Correct answer: a)Olga Korbut

5) Who is the athlete who set the track speed record at the Olympic Games?

Correct answer: a)Usain Bolt

6) Who is the greatest basketball player in the history of the Olympic Games?

Correct answer: d)Gheorghe Mureșan

7) Who is the first athlete to win five gold medals at the Olympic Games?

Correct answer: d)Larisa Latynina

8) Where was the first Olympic stadium built for the modern Games?

Correct answer: a)Athens, Greece

9) Who is the first Arab woman to win an Olympic gold medal?

Correct answer: a)Nawal El Moutawakel

10) Which athlete has won a gold medal without an opponent at the Olympic Games?

Correct answer: d)Walkover in Cricket, 1900

11) Who is the marathon runner who ran and won without shoes?

Correct answer: b)Abebe Bikila

12) Which rugby team holds the record for the fastest win?

Correct answer: (d)France

13) Who is the swimmer who broke the world record while wearing jeans?

Correct answer: d)Fred Bousquet

14) What was the day the Olympic Games conquered the world?

Correct answer: a)Opening of the Athens Games in 1896

15) Who is the first African team to win a gold medal at the Olympic Games?

Correct answer: d)Nigeria national football team, 1996

16) Who is the first Paralympic mascot?

Correct answer: d)Schneemann

17) What is the record for the longest ski jump in history?

Right answer: c)251.5m

18) When did ice hockey become an Olympic discipline?

Correct answer: b)1920

19) When were the Paralympic Games officially recognized?

Correct answer: a)1960

20) Which team has won a competition without even playing?

Correct answer: c)Great Britain Cricket Team, 1900

Printed in Great Britain
by Amazon

36620469R00066